Slack Action

SLACK ACTION

POEMS

Jeffery Donaldson

The Porcupine's Quill

Library and Archives Canada Cataloguing in Publication

Donaldson, Jeffery, 1960–, author
    Slack action : poems / Jeffery Donaldson.

ISBN 978-0-88984-367-7 (pbk.)

    I. Title.

PS8557.O527S53 2013   C811'.54   C2013-903849-3

Published by The Porcupine's Quill, 68 Main Street, PO Box 160,
Erin, Ontario NOB 1TO. http://porcupinesquill.ca

Readied for the press by Amanda Jernigan.

Represented in Canada by Canadian Manda Group.
Trade orders are available from University of Toronto Press.

We acknowledge the support of the Ontario Arts Council and the
Canada Council for the Arts for our publishing program. The
financial support of the Government of Canada through the
Canada Book Fund is also gratefully acknowledged.

Canada Council   Conseil des Arts
for the Arts   du Canada

ONTARIO ARTS COUNCIL
CONSEIL DES ARTS DE L'ONTARIO

Ontario Media Development
Corporation

For my father
Harold James Donaldson

and in memory of my mother
Barbara Joyce Donaldson
1934–2011

Table of Contents

Slack Action

Toy Poems

House of Cards

Slack Action

Lift

Here's a nightmare you may recognize.
An elevator, summoned, opens wide.
You find it empty, welcoming enough.
Muzak and lambent lights. You step inside

and press its buttons, trusting a machine
to find your proper level. In a mood
of measured poise you bide your time,
slightly embarrassed by the solitude.

But stop! There's no surprising bump,
no warning by alarm, save that the doors,
somehow having ideas of their own,
have opened between two floors.

Why so frightened? Cables, backup brake
will keep you pendant, safe from the abyss,
but you bang at buttons and you pinch yourself.
You've never yet felt paralyzed like this.

A host of last illusions falls away.
You see the flapping cables on the wall,
you see cement unpainted, pipes and clamps,
you see the switch box and electrical,

the side-rail wheels extending from your car,
a ladder even for the climbing free,
illuminated as they never are
by your being where you shouldn't be.

You've done it now, you think, and close your eyes,
and dream of empty space, above, below,
those inner soundings, silent and unseen.
You're chilled to think that they were always so,

and rode along to keep them out of mind.
The devil's perch of walled-in promontories
gives views of nothing you can recognize
when doors don't open on familiar storeys.

You lurch awake and shudder, gaze about.
Your room is a warm, illuminated box
with windows on all sides and distant views.
The sunlight in the fields, the meadow walks

drift placidly away from where you look
down at them from above in broken tiers,
a sense of lift lowering through the downs
to stop as on a landing, like a stairs.

Slack Action

It goes through my mind like a train at night,
the train my father rode in the night, his mind
a train of thought far from where he rode.

When I pull into the seniors' home I like to feel
the car drift in abeyance round the last corner,
another touch to come nearer, the braking slide

into parking easements and an end. Forty-two
years he leapt among the tracks, nights, to cobble
things together, shuffling boxcars and flat cars,

dealing their lengths part way into sidings—join
and hinge, muster and release—climbing the ladders
free of his uncouplings. It took some sorting out.

He listened hard for the word come down
from the Dispatcher. Too heavy now for the staff,
he has to wait for the machine that will hoist him,

strapped, over to his chair or back to bed again.
A sandbag, his sullen mass slumps into the lift
and rises sloppy and unresisting. He goes with it

staring in disbelief. I am borne here. For us,
mother and wife are let go, the love-ties
grappled loose in unbroken entanglements,

our new solitudes gathering and fanning out.
When the sliding door whispers open for me
—in hand his double-double and an apple fritter,

unlooked-forward-to, like a pill that you take—
I enter with purpose but am halfway off again.
Our family is convergence and divergence both.

I have a photograph of him in mind, a man
in his prime leaning out from the boxcar's ladder,
signalling ahead the slow recessions, the gaps

and clearances, the thrown switches and coupler
knuckles ... ten feet and closing, five feet, good.
His grief looks poor on him. Plan was he'd be

the first to go—with drinks and smokes, half by
his own wishing—and Mum's years would ease
ahead of him by whole decades. But after

Alzheimer's and a kidney ache, her body still shining
with something fifty about it went off and left him
cajoling his clogged arteries past eighty and beyond.

We never spoke of this, but I always imagined
those seemingly endless trains he assembled
in the night, a hundred cars and counting,

how, when the engine pulls up a little
and the cars buckle forward in succession
but have not yet stopped before the hogger guns it,

it must be that all the fastenings along
let up in turn and spread fresh gaps throughout.
Cars and clusters of cars at once go

clutching and unclutching down their length.
And I try to picture how, the jolting instress
unravelling, their reciprocal momentums

would meet and intermingle, the forward push
backing into slows, and the slows pulling off
pulling forward ahead of their kickbacks and jostles,

and you would hear the whole thing down the line
at once parting and gathering, the entire train
getting on, undecided. But how too, if you really

listened for it, there would be single cars hidden
in the midst, scudding alone, neither pushed
nor pulled, left gentled into hiatus, coasting free

an instant in the long line's accordion folds'
uneasy breathing. A hovering out of waiting,
the glide getting on in the inertia, itself still moving.

He comes to with a jolt. I take in my stride
his pantomimed 'Look who it is!' and we embrace,
our private journeys sallying up behind us

in opposite directions, gently coupling. Not
a greeting or farewell, but a staying that is
neither between us. He keeps me close, and not

to come undone, I tell him what I've been
thinking about the train. 'Slack action, it's called,'
he says, and lets his arms fall open around me.

Assisted Care

Tears at the thought of moving. Failing health.
Your God was ganging up on you. And us?
The word was *proper care*. We acted in good faith.

The room they found you had a gurney bed,
two windows, blinded, on an empty yard,
a table for a picture by your head.

The hurt buried in Old English *caru*
would bide its time, while Old Norse French
slipped backwards through *cura*'s 'taking care'

to waken Latin's *caritas* lament
(that almost by itself holds all things dear),
but that the hearty Anglo-Saxon grunt

turns everything to suffering and grief.
We closed the door on your 'Assisted Care',
a helping of sorrow beyond belief.

Inspirit

I

Nothing stirring. Snow-thaw and dirty fog
at the wide windows dawning on all sides.
Inaudible ice water globing under the eaves.

Plates and cups aimlessly tidied up,
teapot wintering in its quilted cozy.
My sisters. Myself. The morning vigil,

not any longer for our mother's passing
in a world she had not been dying to leave,
but for denouement and the stillness after.

Quiet as candles left burning by day,
we listen and think each of us alone
(after or before, does it even matter?)

of the ways that those who would leave us
linger, and return to us afresh in new forms,
moving among us, there and not there.

'Inspirit Residence' the home is called,
whose inhabitants' withdrawing dementias
mock at 'Retirement with Assisted Care'.

A hush descends on the empty rooms,
as after any loss, closets full of clothes
for sending off the moment we can face

the added grief, the piecemeal giving parts
of her away (sooner, we are urged, than later),
the bedroom door still shut for keeping safe

(please until the later spring?) the phantom
we find so impatient to be wandering.
She could linger like this for another year

the social workers warn, her fading memory
is but a conjuring out of hurt, daily visitations
from unreachable depths, a wakelessness.

Once more, we feel a stirring in the room,
and there it is again, as most mornings
since the day we had first lost her,

a worried presence drifting aimlessly,
the smiling recognition, the soft-edged ghost
of my mother's face, her eyes watering

with expectation and that loving look that each
dawn spilled from her as welcome, as though
you were back, waking, from long travels.

Her old self still, pale to transparency.
And then, again, the sudden look of doubt
that follows, her eyes questioning the room

for common hints, a memory of this place
she has walked into somehow unknowingly
from another world. We brace ourselves.

II

It was something that Hamlet knew deep down,
but didn't know he knew, didn't remember
that he hadn't forgotten. He needed reminding.

No wonder his father's ghost scared that oath
out of him. Not every day you get to watch
the cantankerous old man crash around

in full armour like a drunken pot salesman.
And not himself either, bearing nothing
but bad news about this world and the next one.

But then what did Hamlet expect? High fives
and a bear hug? There was hard business afoot.
Criminal losses. The poor spook was miffed,

wailed on about a wayward wife tupped daily
by the villain that stiffed him. Hamlet listened,
and it spelled the end of *steady as she goes*.

Yet I wonder who was most haunted there.
Parent or child? The nasty lab brew went
straight to the king's brains and froze him out.

Can we even think how that must have felt?
Your noggin ossified in stucco strips,
vile and loathsome crust, synaptic through-puts

numbed to stone, where loves once lived,
its neurons cleaved, names and faces
snowbound in their dark dwellings, the wires down.

Appearing ghosts are spirits of unknowing.
Arms extended, they grope their own next thoughts,
their minds drained of argument and purpose.

The spirit turned, and his fading exhortation
to recall left for Hamlet's further brooding
a brief mnemonic, that loss itself of memory

is more a crime than any quicker death, its recompense,
a begged word or deed altogether different
than revenge. Hamlet went mad trying to think of it.

III

She stepped into the light where we could see her.
Nightgown and furry slippers, shin-pegs white
and waxy as baking paper, hair matted

from another bad night. An air of drifting
in circles around a purgatory's musical-chairs
played out to nobody's tuneless accompaniment.

Her eyes passed over me, gathered focus,
and looked, not so much knowing me by name,
but as though she had grown tired of waiting

and now wished to speak, still circumspect
and untrusting. 'List. List! Where's that damned
list. My children will be here in hours

and I have shopping to do. I've nothing
to cook, and the house is a disaster.'
She smoothed out an imaginary skirt.

'Your children, yes!' I tried to go along.
'Those no-good ingrates, hardly ever here.
I'm amazed at them. But it's all arranged.'

She scowled at that, worked her tongue and jaw
as though she tasted something dry,
then fell upon another thought. 'Oh horrible!

I'm late for work. You left me to sleep in!
I'll have to rush,' now reaching to her head
to fix a phantom nursing cap and pin.

We stared blankly at the cooling teapot,
its frayed, hand-knitted purple yarn
closing around the sides like open hands

that bend to cup cold cheeks just in from snow.
She raised her eyes, dim with afterthought,
and made as though to speak, but let it fall,

worn out, if not with love, then with a brain
each day more hardened against it, and turned
instead back towards where she'd come from,

as though the story she was here to tell of shady
ends were old news now, even to herself,
remembered in spirit, if not in fact, leaving her

these mornings to go from us like this, each time
for real, we in her wake loving to bring her back.
By heaven, I'll make a ghost of her that lets me.

Hand

A four-inch plate of fossil clay
fired by kiln. My handprint made
when I was five, an ashen grey
glazed at 800 centigrade.

Around the edges painted red,
a green lace threaded through a hole
brought back around, a finger knot,
as though I'd something to recall.

Kindergarten's first day come,
you must have had my hand in yours
the whole way through, for I still feel
('The coat rack's here. Let go the doors!

Now don't be silly, Jeff. Be brave,
I'll be right back before you know.
Miss Nelson here will take you in'),
the moment when you let it go.

I see the countertop, damp clay.
My fingers closed together firm,
I pressed down hard and made for you
a desperate, hopeless, keeping charm.

Now years go by, the hand turns up,
a disembodied, severed palm
inside your white ash jewellery box,
fingering paper clips and balm,

as though an offering in kind
that grasped a boy's tenacious will,
attached to no one now around,
meant something to you still.

Lie down now in this wooden box
(you'll not be back before I know),
and I will give you back this hand
for you to hold, your fingers so,

pressed together firm on mine
the whole way through ('We can't begin ...
the flowers here, the cards ... to say
how loved ...'), and I will take you in.

And once the kiln is fired, we'll go
and make of clay on clay one flesh
of keepsakes and assorted gifts
inside a jewellery box of ash.

The Contents

A child is born, stands up, looks fore and aft,
wonders how he got to be, in time,
and questions how it's he inside himself
instead of someone else. Gestalt sublime.

I know that feeling of existential hurt,
the intuition that our animus
is not our own. Or even harder dirt,
that we are only accidentally us.

But think now. How in heaven could it be
that a living child's mindful properties
break loose and fall adrift, become at sea,
foundering in shallow waters. Please.

What we need's a dose of common sense.
Send the child outside to find a stone
and mind not any stone, one plumb and dense
that carries all its contents on its own.

Now have him turn it, pat it with his hand.
Inside and out it's hard, as hard as stone.
Just sand in sand in sand in sand in sand.
Container and contained are simply one.

That you are you is no great puzzlement.
Stone's just being stone's its *being as*.
It could no more be other element
than other things themselves. That's how it is.

Hard comfort, yes. But mysteries are such
that howsoever stone as stone congeals,
notice how the child's canny touch
is curious to find out how it feels.

Eocene Plant Fossil

For Miller

Brief summer, you are a touchstone
under glass, a gloss on yourself.

Forty million years is a big number
when you think of it. But give it

enough time and it will pass.
You measure how long things go on.

You are the signature of a certain
vanished October, its deep shadows

and its photosynthesis, the noise
of crickets at night, this single leaf

unrising onto its shadow,
a certain hour, a certain moment.

You should be nothing but an archetype,
a likeness, as though what you held

in keeping were but the *sort* of leaf
we might once have found

before the living summer hardened.
But your markings are intimidating.

Petiole. Midrib. Vein.
I have never seen such perfect detail.

And I suppose that must be why
you could never let leaves make

impressions like this on us.
We would end up living forever.

With a Line from a Dream

A page of poetry on the table.
It is like a child bending down
and placing a hand on the earth
to find out what it weighs.

Four Haiku

Oath

Born only to die.
This is the last time I'll fall
for that old fast one.

•

On a Road in Winter

Bird feeder, mailbox:
abandoned readinesses
to give and receive.

•

Rock Point

This palmed shale's too plumb,
but almost heart-shaped enough,
to skip on water.

•

Search

Google 'oracle'.
What does the priestess not know
to answer? Don't ask.

Troy

Eight centuries before
the common era, outside
the walls of a later Troy,

toy merchants hawked models
of the Trojan Horse,
and the children cried for them.

Centuries earlier, the gates
of Ilium were breached
when the colossal toy,

rumbling, was trotted in,
a winner's trophy, almost a gift,
until from the underside

spilled the tin soldiers
who cut open the children
crying inside the walls.

The Stadium

In the stadium were all those from town
who had died. The Great Reunion had come at last.

It was evening and the stadium lights brightened
slowly under the dusk that was peaceful and cool.

The flags were raised on the light standards along
the boulevards, and the libraries and banks were closed.

There was a light breeze in the park. The townspeople
from every quarter pressed onto the bleachers

looking out among the absent ones below them:
the much missed and the forgotten, the far too young,

those who were lost by accident, those who took leave
by their own act, and the longsuffering elderly

who at the end dreamed they were falling asleep,
and those who died under an angry hand.

Many in the bleachers cried out to single ones by name,
gesticulating wildly, though for all that

their loved ones failed to notice and more often
than not simply looked the wrong way.

Besides there were so many calling. The dead
held hands and huddled together and watched

with a blinking innocence as of children woken
in the small hours to witness an eclipse of the moon.

When it was almost dark, a bell rang in the bell tower,
and all heads turned alike to the poet who came down

slowly from the bleachers and stepped up to the podium
unfolding a single paper, and paused, and read aloud

a poem he had written specially for the occasion,
though it was hard to hear, as many later commented,

over the general hum that persisted the whole time.
The poet held the paper down in the breeze.

Then the ceremony ended and there was a word
of thanks, and the people began to leave,

some eagerly, some looking back, but all filing
quietly into the boulevards of the town

where the name above the diner flickered on again,
and where, had you looked from above,

you would have seen homes light up one by one
along the avenues the way stars come out at dusk.

The poet was gone. The poem he had read
was about a toy he had lost when he was a child.

The dead stood in the stadium and looked about them.
They had not been asked to leave or stay.

More than Thirteen Ways
of Looking at a Listener

Listeners at a reading
are like waves rolling to shore.
They stop in front of it.

Listeners at a reading
are like the echoes of a bucket
in the depths of the well.

Listeners at a reading
are like a person who mistakes
a shelter for a bus stop
where you wait for buses.

Listeners at a reading
are like a dog sitting by its master.
The master is talking to someone.
The dog stares into the fire.

Listeners at a reading
are like frisky retrievers.
They run to fetch what you throw.
They sometimes give up and lie down.

Listeners at a reading
are mirrors in the morning
you try not to look into.

Listeners at a reading
are bums in seats.

Listeners at a reading
are like the winter bough
on which a bird sits and sings.

Listeners at a reading
are like the soup ladle
beside a pot of soup.

Listeners at a reading
are like a chair found
in the middle of the woods.

Listeners at a reading
are like the forest a tree falls in
when there is someone there.

Listeners at a reading
are like the poet's worst nightmare,
still there after he sits bolt upright.

Listeners at a reading
are like girls at a wedding.
The poet throws her bouquet.

The poem is a communion wafer.
Listeners at a reading
open their mouths.

Listeners at a reading are like a day
in late September, the Bruce Trail
on the escarpment near Grimsby

after the leaves have begun turning
and the air has a sour nip
because it rained that morning

and the colours are deeper
and richer than on the dry days,
and I can see the lake

off through the trees below me
with its heavy blue all the way out
and I keep still for a moment

and there is nothing like a wind
and you can hear a leaf drop
for there isn't a sound

and without a sound I cannot tell
without looking, whether I am
the listener at a reading, or it is.

The Selected Poems

Make of your life's work one book of poems
of middling length: a hopeful eighty-five,
counting years as pages? Not of course the tomes
of record when Noah was alive,

but respectable enough by modern measure.
Read on. The toddlering early pages.
In wobbling lines you find your feet, pleasure
your language through the potty stages,

when the odd smelly one, not laid aside,
is seen as cute, greeted with smiles
of grimaced understanding if not pride.
And your teens? The trying on of styles

when every syllable is a bold cravat,
indubitably polished and urbane,
the clip-on kind of course, soon bristled at
once folded loopings happen on their own.

One needs an ear of granite not to wince
at yak as glib in its naiveté
as it is brash. Thus modestly convinced
of your lasting genius, you think one day

they'll quote your lines in English 105;
the world neglected them at its peril.
You are holding up the Canadian side,
at least as good as Auden or James Merrill.

Flit through the middle pages at your ease.
Listen for the genuine creation
that rustles in erotic pleasantries
and the least verbal ejaculation,

and find to your surprise, as Hopkins said,
you cannot breed even one work that wakes.
Among unwatered roots, you seek the dead
in antiphonal plagiaries and fakes.

At 50, that caveat of Robert Lowell,
that the eye will see what the hand has done,
makes Yeats's 'Dialogue of Self and Soul'
(unbearable lightness!) weigh a ton.

When to have chosen any tack or beat
no matter how remote, circuitous,
points up a road not taken, past your art.
But then you get to thinking, nonetheless,

that if you plan to have a final break
of summary aplomb, best have it soon:
that metaphor, as sedulous as weak,
of starting out, such as you are, again.

And even if the feet no longer dance,
you find the page itself is numinous:
a scuffling foil, a stave, a wrinkled face,
insisting on a niche, if nowhere else,

at least within the margins there enclosed
to bear in bold defence of fictive work
the artful apologia of those
whose names are writ across a watermark.

Towards 85 you find the leaves uncut.
Never mind a villanelle or sonnet,
you're glad to glimpse ahead, no matter what,
any page with something written on it.

For round which unturned verso, out of sight,
you cannot tell as yet, white pages stir,
where the pencilled doodlings of whoever-might
will decorate your last blank signature.

Now close, and as you gather dust, face down,
don't hide those grudging blurbs your buddies owed,
for the rest is a two-line bio at the end,
and fame a Universal Product Code.

A Touretter's Twelve-Tone Sonnet

The glib angle's soffit gables true.
Chaff saddleback, the aster's alms.
The woodlot's whistle and jib.
When the fickle mastiff ails,
Judge Gumdrop is armless.
Four thrums jangle a thyroid.
Cankers' white over sibilance.
Murphy grit. Oslo's napper.
Fetid umbrage gambles sturgeon.
The cinder's affable mug
Is meddling by plaster bristles.
Sedge for mixing Ollie's jester.
Hobbled imp. Plumb's icky nat.
Tongue luck.

Toy Poems

Jack-in-the-Box

Always the same old tune, the rote
lessons of form versus content
you keep trying to get a lid on.

Inside, a lurking presence. Outside,
a music to rattle it out by the one
handle, the inner expression sprung

in truth from its own trappings.
Your buried clown gathered to itself,
head lowered, scheming, its revelation

a joke. Maybe it has got too easy
these last years. Just crank up
the old Tourettic jangler, and pop!

out with it! a top-heavy doddering
expression's gangling hysteria, joyful
as all get-out. The very idea!

No wonder you've always
looked askance at what's inside.
But why play then? Did you think

your wound-up loping strains kept
the bounder at bay? Why,
it's the cranking that stirs him!

Or you just thought it would sound
better, and that you wouldn't flinch
like this every time around.

Spinning Top

A line goes round and round inside,
collects itself, and holds to a single end
hung loose for getting grips. You pull

and put some English on it, the binding
ravel of its own accord unravels free
and the strung turns, unleashed, whip

loose of the inner stay's unlengthenings.
That makes the head spin for starters.
The top-heavy upshot, weighing the lift,

gathers to a pitch, and its untoppled peak
thrown centripetal steadies on a point.
It makes fast and hangs there a moment,

polished, dashing, upright in spite of itself,
a radiance drawn from inside evened out,
shedding its own sway, its give,

to stand an instant plumb. You feel the gist
straight up, but no sooner hold its easement
augural of the spinner's sound character,

than it slowly wobbles into roundabouts;
the spilled momentums, unbuoyed, lose track
of their own slant, trace out widening

sphere on sphere of illegible doodlings,
until the veering foot—uplift akilter,
its roundings all but spent—throws a failing

sidelong pirouette onto its own shadow
and touches down. Dull rocking, small wonder,
now that the gracious equilibrium is over.

I would do it all again if there was time.
But look, here is the trailing line I first tried
out of hand to pull off clear away. Have a go.

Yo-yo

This should be easy to handle: descent
and ascent, down and up, fall and rise.
Resurrection motif. Harrowing of hell.

And all the potential of catastrophe.
Writing about it is like taking candy
from a child. The premise is ready made.

It goes like this: make the simplest
of gestures with your hand, as though
you were explaining something, as though

you were saying 'take this if you like',
and casually opened your fingers. The palmed
trifle long held-to would spill from them.

How some smart spinners get the hang of it
amazes me, certain that every tossed-off
letdown backs up on itself into fallout,

follow-through, its inverse ineluctable:
the redemption, the homecoming, the unravelled
of its own ravelling again. Nothing lost!

It's the whole comeliness of the afterlife:
spin off into the abyss, and use your free
fall for bounce-back, find yourself once more

at hand, ready to go again. A flourish,
a snap. One of the best yarns we have!
They make it seem so easy and intuitive.

They say all you need is the right touch
and a little faith that it will all come about.
But my own efforts are no good omen.

I get defensive. To let go at the wrong time,
I say, to fritter away or bungle the fling,
or lose heart at my own half-taken-back

'take this if you like', sure, may be my own
undoing. But I'm a good sport. If anyone
can do better, I wager there's a trick to it.

Rocking Horse

You run from what you are, sad frolicker,
high horse riderless in the attic corner,
set to the side once the children's playroom

was converted for guests. Getting up there
in years. A flouring of dust feathers your finish,
your silver dapple sun-washed to cinder.

I think of your shape once buried
at the heart of a northern pine. Those years
in the forest, the summers danced rings

around you and the tree grew tall.
That was before the clear-cut cut you clear
and you came off like the Dying Slave

in Michelangelo's unfinished sculpture
writhing free of his own stone footings.
You were cut and split and planed,

and measured two by two for feet, the grain
aligned with your tassel mane's polished nap.
You think the buffed rails are beneath you,

but you ride them out (I can see what bits
run through your head): the way the floating
circles at your feet, the way the bend rises

backward more than forward, and you rear
at the pulling off, and gravity, spurred on,
rolls through its bottoming-out, momentum's

ambit pitching at the brink, the headstrong
throw into urge and impetus, the fallback
easing off into gathering's uplift. The ritual

is trotted out. And because you were built
this way, on run-throughs, on memory's
back-and-forth, you go through them still,

the motions that is, like you were getting
somewhere, and as though the child
you ran with hadn't long since moved on.

Figurine

The small woman upstairs in the dollhouse
fears that she was only made for fun,
a modern parable from the Book of Job.

She sits rigid as the day she was made
by the low-gabled window in the attic,
her vanity nearby with its slanting mirror,

a tiny comb jammed stiffly in her hand.
Never once has she looked out the window.
The roof is gone. Always the same weather.

She lives alone, except on rare days when
out of nowhere someone arrives below
making a noise around the kitchen stove

(where red flames hang motionless as paint),
or appearing later, stood up in the hall,
those times she isn't moved to join him.

She says: 'If only someone nice would come.
Look at me. I'm a perfect doll. I have a mirror
and a comb. I feel certain I was put here.'

She remembers one time it seemed in a dream
she felt the entire house-front swing open
and a light shine, and there was whispering,

and she looked as she imagined into the face
of innocence. Most nights, however,
the evening lamp is turned down and the house

grows still and the stucco stars pay out their fading
incandescent green and below the stairs
the unextinguished fire blackens in the stove,

and the night comes on and before the hour
for bed she recites once more to herself
the mantra she has known from the beginning:

When I was a child, I spoke as a child,
I felt as a child, I thought as a child: now
I am grown, I must put away childish things.

Marbles

My marbles, I lost the damned things years ago.
Been sorry ever since. Kept them safe
in one of those purple whisky bags by Crown Royal.

I was the king of a dominion's bright subjects:
globed iridescences in glass, buffed lustres,
and stirrings inside crystal shape in shape,

ribbon and shawl, nebulae and nimbus,
silk scarves and swirls of DNA flung skyward
in their gelled ethers, clear-eyed experiments

in the origin of colour. Looked at more closely:
cosmologies, every one! Deep space turned
inside out, like pairs of socks, into glassy planets,

their spheres, spin them how you would, folded into
their own waters. All mine! the rings inside Saturn,
Jupiter's swallowed moons. Or turned round

once more, they were inner cells, bright spores
in clouds of unwound mitochondria in their gels,
the nuclei's backward drift, a jellyfish's

undulating wisps. I loved the way the rainbows
and particles bent to the shape of their own element
and found their angles there, the arc and gleam

of each radiant crescent; how everything bathed
in its own lucidity. How even the mists were
clarities, how nothing made to be seen was unseen,

for everything inside them was just out there.
How each one was fixed for good, but how also
for variety there was variety, and how each new

marble in the game changed everything, simply
by adding itself. When they came together
straightforwardly they made a nicking noise

like the sound of stones bunting under water,
harmless and distant. The bubbles went their way,
imperfections floating equally among perfections.

I should know better than to go soft about them.
The time for those pastoral kingdoms is behind us,
says the latest thinking, if there ever was one.

It was how I lost them. If I'd stored them on a top
shelf until I thought to hand them on, that would be
one thing. A day came when they were gone is all.

I loved their dawning candles, their twilights' unbluing
ether tapering when they turned, as though fluorescence
could drain through an hourglass. I've no idea what

became of them, my brilliant auroras, my moons,
my stars of a vast dominion long gone from this empty
head of mine, my purple whisky bag by Crown Royal.

Kite

It's the dull days, the days of empty fields
lying empty like this, no one but you,

and the sky not pulling and the flagging line
loose in your hand, its tensions falling

over themselves into aimless knots,
and the un-upshooting upshot it still

even then unwinds to going nowhere.
Leave it there, turn about and run.

Sprint from the listless dithering,
go from it crosswise and antithetical,

angle off sidelong from the slackening,
fly left and right, haul back and pivot sheer.

Feel the air make way where you dart,
the stillness clear, feel the ambling idler

catch in the wind among the unfathomed
scuds high enough in its own draft it rises

out of hand. Now it has gumption and gist,
the heft of it lagging upwards against you,

your whole weight resting now gone into it.
Hold the line, its heavy sway drawn skyward

so high, in spite of itself, it thins to vanishing,
your dwindling craft poised it almost seems

past its reach in the far-gone strata. Sailing.
Leave it there while you take it in.

Ball

Conjured in space, a sphere
is almost the first thing an object
would think of being.

We tried to follow after,
but kept going in circles,
failed to find our way into it,

or back, to the original oomph
when an idea, full of itself,
thought it could make a point,

said no to a central void
and pulled back from it, found
it was next to nothing in the end.

Which may be why in games
we keep trying to throw it away.
Not this, we say, not this.

But look at the children in the field
laughing and calling.
They run after where it rolls.

Material Cause

If you were a length of northern
pinewood, what would you want to end
up as, if, say, you were given a say?

Would you go for something practical?
The bowl of a deep spoon ladling out
daily soups in a west-end soup kitchen?

The handle of a hammer? A toothpick?
Or subtly authoritative, one of four legs
on the Speaker's chair in parliament?

Almost anything really. What would
you make of having turned out like this,
rocking horse, merely imaginary

for the hell of it, set to work in play,
back and forth, an example of yourself,
or rather an example of what you really

aren't. Would you wonder if real wood
for pretend uses was really pretend wood?
I only ask because I am made of bones.

House of Cards

Game of Marbles

After a while, if there are poets you admire
well enough, you are glad to read them
on anything, just to get their proper aim,

their measure of alignments and configurations,
their bearings inside any given circumference,
how they knuckle down, start from without

and pick their way inward from the margins
with poised scatterings and agile parsings-out
that open up new ways and slants to the interior.

It's watching their entanglements disperse, the route
unknot itself, scramble and spread into gradual
clearances. It's how, if the shooter has any guile,

has lightly flipped each keeper from its place
into new looks and clusters, themselves
unclustering, you are left when the field clears

with a refreshing emptiness. It is as though
the anglers could move each other and themselves
so out of hand that nothing remained in the end

but the original setting apart, the room there was
to play in, where they had picked themselves up,
skrimmed hard after breaking, and skedaddled.

House of Cards

For Garry Sherbert

Ah, that fine fragile cathedral,
said Jacques Derrida of Northrop Frye's
Anatomy, one evening he was asked,

and there implied that, sooner or later,
literature's whole top-heavy elaborate estate,
its fictive papers gingerly assembled,

would come crashing down on itself,
your canny devotions notwithstanding.
Said Frye himself: *the world we create*

in our imaginations is above time;
when the whole structure is finished,
nature, its scaffolding, is knocked away....

For Monsieur, there is fiction's ephemera,
the broad-footed obelisk's weightless
undergirdings, giddy and unhinged.

For the Canuck, *nature* is the provisional
gizmo, down and out, all gauze and gimcrack,
a mustered rigging's trial-and-error.

Something between them will have to give.
Look this way and let us watch a moment
this child at work on a house of cards,

her painstaking piecemeal agglomerations,
rows of card-pair tepees' touching tips
rising pyramidal, fine-flicked and unquibbling,

frangible as Tiffany. Her gangly,
jeweller's-eye-tuned hand at widdershins
and dodging round buttresses athwart

must have a knack for stealth, that furtive
gesture, nearly, of not putting a thing
where you leave it, lifting your fingers free.

The testy habiliments climb to a single point,
lightheaded, slackening upwards,
all the more shouldering less and less,

next to nothing in the end. Fixed on little
more than the touchy gossamer integrals,
she knows its equilibrium is a travesty,

how far from sound-footed, how possessed
of no greater poise than that each
tipped ligature is already half-toppled.

And she knows how we wait for hubris
to carry it off the moment she gingers
a last card onto the ticklish pinnacle.

How that last one didn't trigger the upset
letdown already settled upon, who knows?
Her patience is dizzying. Her fingers, feathers.

In the end she will not keep us guessing,
or leave unproven for a Derrida or Frye
what comes next once she is finished with it,

this dwelling she had a hand in making
that tapers at all odds above the fallen world,
once she is above knocking it down.

Magic Lantern

It replaced the opacity of walls with impalpable
iridescences, supernatural multicoloured
apparitions, where legends were depicted
in a wavering, momentary, stained-glass window.

— Marcel Proust

Powerpoint is the new Allegory of the Cave,
fictive facts, the silver coin of the realm.
I'm still at it, pitching from the back room

transparent illusions that keep young eyes
looking ahead. That's me at the front
of the lecture theatre, piercing the heart

of one more elaborate conceit with the false
confidence of a red laser's penetrating point.
The slide projectors of my day have gone digital.

Emily Dickinson's poems are annunciations;
they glint like a messenger's angelic forecast,
three hundred virgin readers still in the dark.

Milton's prayer to the muse is shining through.
Another remote gesture, and the opening lines
of Arnold's 'Dover Beach' gleam and are gone.

Naturally there were no bulbs in the oldest ones,
which worked by an oil lamp's jaundiced candlelight,
its metal box like a miniature stove furnace

stuck to a lens, before whose single focus passed
stills motioning in the lustres of unfolding myths
and allegories all a-swim. You can still find them

in the flea markets. Have you ever seen one?
It is in watching how the candle burns that you see
the light. A solitary flame waffles and dithers

in drinks of air, unsure of itself, wavering like a slip
of underwater grass's unctuous twirls, doddering
in its flickers. And where the image falls ahead,

on the doorknob, by the window, you see something
moving in the glow, tapered, dissimulating,
pulling up short of its own diffident semblances.

You see how light, ghostly and metamorphic,
can falter where it falls and be there still, its images
borne like fish glimpsed in water, taken aback.

But really nothing like these lessons in Powerpoint,
where the lumens burn hot, burn out. Which is why,
when I turn to the remote, and the words go slanting

and musing with Dickinson or Milton, I think
of the lantern's inherent reserve, its illuminations
on the verge of going out, ticklish and mercurial,

how they hardly dare skim the surface of things
more brightly than they do, and show something
not really there hidden in the light that bears it.

It must be why in lecture at the screen I find myself
sometimes dancing my awkward two-step out in front,
nearly blinded by those fictions as a matter of fact,

bending around me in space and washing over me,
those old illuminators, those colourful go-betweens,
kindled shades that stand now for their vanishing.

Kite Metaphor

Because the air is empty and because
the emptiness moves over you toward
the west, it can be a comfort to float

something out in it like this, drifters
to pull at and watch climb against their own
bent into the buffs and billows of vacancy.

You think of backbone and vertigo.
But really, that's what metaphor does,
properly speaking. On one end, you,

holding the gathered line ready to run out
on the first bellow, the plunge's
slam, the drag away from you and off.

On the other end: a vehicle, sufficiently
far from where you stand to gap down
the interstice and hold the tension taut,

grab at your give when you least expect.
Call it, this go-round (and for lack
of a better lark) Baudelaire's albatross,

that lumbering heightener, vast sails akimbo,
too big by far to sweep unentangled through
our mundane vernacular, telling it like it is

until the trapped rigging loosens it undone
into the void distances, lugging the clear
surge and hauling whims backwards

through the exhausted essence, with you here
on the ground, keeping up by holding it
down. The kite, that is, if you must know.

Correspondences

— Charles Baudelaire

Nature is a monument to itself, an open book.
Its leaves are aflutter with all it would say,
but it keeps to itself, spies you on your way
in forests of dark totems, with a knowing look.

It echoes its likenesses, distant and near
in the fallen dark, at one with themselves
and big as the night. You sense rising clear
the sounding-within of all colours and smells.

The almond incense of a newborn's fleece,
a meadow's green breath, woodwinds at dusk,
contend with rank spoilage, rich, in your face,

until the drift of it all, the whole, opens wide,
and the balm of amber and the gist of musk
get carried away in your dumbfounded head.

An Honest Man

This nostalgia for the origin of experience,
it wears you down but keeps sending you out
once more to get the knack of the evening

in the narrow streets before the evening passes.
And the evening passes and you come back
to where you started, not in time, for it is

later now, but to the place, to the doorway
you parted from, its barn wood still faded blue
the way you left it. Another let-down.

You keep feeling, in spite of yourself, that there is
an openness about the windows that you can
see through, and a scent under the clotheslines

not made from other scents. And yet how far
these mayhaps must be from their earliest
forms and templates, the evening's archetypal jig.

There is the story of the man who went out
one evening to find it, the primordial pattern,
the evening that had been used since the beginning

to make other evenings, and he carried a lighted
lantern as they say Diogenes once did when
the sun was still shining. He held it out in front.

And people thought it was odd the way he looked,
as he walked out beyond the end of the village
where the road turned and the streetlights fell away.

And the story has it that he failed like the others,
that once the sun had gone out on the horizon
he came back through the village streets in the dark

with nothing to show for his long excursion,
no branch or stone, no souvenir, nor any news
of the clouds and where they had come from.

Except that the lamp was gone, left somewhere
in the fields, you imagine, pointless there,
but easy enough to find before daybreak.

Open

The field was his favourite place
to go walking, where he thought
of the path in the yellow grass

as a metaphor for getting on with things.
It went up into the broken hills
to a stand of trees and a wide view.

For a long time he had believed
that going out was the key.
His master key was just being there.

Its cut notches and bevels
fit any groove you could name,
and with an easy turn unlocked

the unspoken ways he hadn't found yet,
ways that were closed to others.
He would see what they opened to.

But as time passed and he moved
forward, he saw that his key
was not the one he had in mind,

that his was a single key, carved
with bevels and ridges that were
only his own, always the same ones

that anyone could guess were his,
cut the same way that opened
only one lock always the same.

And it was then that he saw
that all around him there were
locks still locked against him,

locks he hadn't seen because
he didn't have the key,
locks of every shape and size,

every contour, every depth,
that the key to open them was ...
but he didn't know what it was.

After that he thought differently
about the path into the hills
that only grew clearer as it rose.

It was the only way open to him,
he knew that now, and nothing
open to him would show the way.

II

There was a field he pictured in his mind,
his favourite place to go and think.
He smiled and thought of the path

cleared in the yellow grass as a metaphor
for making poems, how he was always
finding new ways to move forward in them.

In his mind it gave onto the hills
to a stand of trees and a view beyond them,
a view that he had not yet seen,

but thought he could, any time he liked,
as he made his way up to them.
His mind was the key, thinking ahead.

Its bent fit any groove you could name,
and with an easy turn unlocked
doors along the way he hadn't found yet,

ways that were closed to others.
Only he would see what they opened to.
But then one day he realized, moving

where he moved, that keys were superfluous.
The doors were already open and simply
gave way when he thought about them.

He must find the door, he imagined,
that was locked and wouldn't open
for anyone, and for which no key existed.

Yet everything he saw was open,
even the paths forward that showed the way.
So he began to think about turning back.

He would just give up and go, he thought,
and drop the key that he had in mind.
And this would be the last time, if he had a say,

he said to himself, that he would think
of the path gone up through the familiar hills
as a way into his unwritten poems,

or as a way of getting anywhere at all,
to the view beyond anywhere at all,
or to the door not there in front of it.

When Things Are Looking Up

I wish the clouds would just say
what they mean and get on with it.
But no, they're all 'Don't mind us,

we're only the fraying magnitudes,
heading east, and have little if anything
to pass along. It's why we keep moving.'

And sure enough, there to the west,
out of the blue more of them are coming,
with brief, uncloudy spaces between them.

A small one catching up says, 'Look to the sky
ahead of us, how it tries to stay clear
and open to gather us in. Go east yourself

and look up, see how it would be, if,
gone ahead, you could say everything
that came to you without thinking.'

Donkey's Way

It would be not quite so bad if we had a place
to keep this good, the original *bittersweet*
of standing in the field this morning,
the spring light sorting out its green laundry,

where the breeze, always heading off,
tells of odours in other fields miles away,
and I can pick out their parts and name them:
the deer grass is thin, the timothy is brown.

Naturally, the breeze has no mind of its own
for these borne spices or the names they bear.
Doesn't need one of course, there being
a creature in its midst with a nose for them.

Pity there is nowhere to put it. This grief
and the memory of it dies when I do.
Nothing around me in which to set it down,
nothing with a lid on it to keep it safe.

There is that scene in Milne's *Winnie the Pooh*
when Eeyore receives two personal gifts
that were spoiled before they got to him:
an empty honey jar and a burst balloon.

Thinking a moment, his riches already ruined,
he drops the balloon gently inside the jar
and then removes it, puts it in, takes it out again,
because it is his birthday, and the givers are sad.

November 5th

I went out into the street to meet the people there.
It was November 8th. I said to them,
but what has happened to November 5th?

We did that one, they said. And I asked,
what, all of you? And they said yes. I scratched
my head: do you mean to say that this is

not happening on November 5th? Nope,
they said. That's how it works. Things happen
on the days that were named for them.

And I said, how's that? And they said, well,
what did you think? And I asked, but what if
there were things on November 5th

that haven't happened yet, how would they
happen now? They laughed and said,
it would be a little late for that, wouldn't it.

I said, how can you live like that?
And they said, water under the bridge,
my friend. And I wanted to say that that

was a cop-out, but asked instead, and today?
They said today is November 8th,
today we do things—I think I get it, I said.

They said, look, we can see this is hard for you,
come back tomorrow and we'll talk about it
some more. I said I would try to be here.

Two on Bonnard

I

His studio wall in Le Cannet,
eight feet of Mediterranean light,
paintings tacked all over on it

wherever he could fit them,
like notes on a cork board.
A ladder for the higher ones.

Some yellow going, he would spot it,
here on a storm cloud's under-quilt,
there for the teacup's glinting node

three pictures over, a gold brilliance
on the *baignoire*'s blue-tiled floor,
the eyes of a cat in the garden.

A general becoming, gradual
bricolage, everything emerging
into its own with everything else.

I wish I could write like that.
Three flicks in the water glass,
and his brush was clean.

II

My daybook is filled
with appointments I'm bound
to forget. Not his.

Each numbered square
filled with quick sketches
of things he had seen:

a goat's head, a tree,
someone reading at a table,
a woman, two boats

at anchor, a lighthouse.
And jotted above them,
a word about the weather.

Beau. Nuageux.
Nothing about deadlines,
or somewhere he had to be,

just the space of a day
filled with pictures
of what goes inside it.

Sweet Talk

This will just take a minute. So there
are these three shells, past, present, and future,
and the guess-where-it-is switcheroo

we like to play with them. For what it's worth,
put a something under the middle one.
Start with the fiat that goes without saying

to keep an eye on it. Now watch carefully.
A dazzling shuffle, a froth of cones,
the trickster's uncoiling spillage

skrimming in half circles over and round,
until each one jumbles in sly among
the other two. You lose track of course,

end up guessing where it is—where *what* is?—
turn over an empty one trying to find it.
Well, a lesson learned. It ought to be easier,

when, for the time being, you reading this now
are the hidden keepsake unloseable
for obvious reasons. Funny that it isn't.

At the Garden of Eden
Thrift Shop and Exchange

They, looking back, all the eastern side beheld
Of Paradise, so late their happy seat,
Waved over by that flaming brand; the gate
With dreadful faces thronged and fiery arms.

— Paradise Lost

Under the entranceway's bright-green awning
and marquee (whose ribbing slogan—
'And you thought Paradise was Lost!'

—winks at all scrabblers after the harmless steal),
face to face unflinching, the security pillars
form a narrow gate and stand firm beyond

the cashier's angelic and unwatchful eye
in mechanical vigilance: keepers
of an unseen static fire, heralds hell-bent

on trumpeting departures. Always
more poker-faced than the Queen's guards,
they know more about you than you think.

Why do you always hesitate going through,
hold back, give yourself a mental strip-search
inside and out, the head-to-foot once-over?

Your credit's fine, and if there's new baggage,
that last account can prove you've settled up.
Or so you think. Buzzers go off in the mind.

The loves badly ended, early anxious lies,
more hurt given than got, the weak word
settled for in awkward need, pretendings

tested for each saving face, untrue lines
of character, the selfish, selfless cosmetic
applied as suited every failing purpose.

And buried in the midst of all, your psyche's
hitched-up, rarely flashed unmentionables,
the pull of hanging figs caught up in

(you wished!) a tempting serpent's wily turns,
sly-handed uprisings you had grappled
all those years to keep in their proper place.

You'll be there all day emptying those pockets.
Like you need another metaphor for guilt. Look.
The lean priests are at the point of reckoning.

Their private listening screen's hot ears
are cocked for every shopper's last confession.
But that trumpet blast—you thought you would die

if you ever heard it—is really the last judgement
you need to worry about. To hell with it. You need
to own that shit. Grab your goods and go.

Express Checkout

The man in line ahead of me at the grocery
had died years ago. He was still the same,

bony shoulders, hands of a pianist,
sandals with socks. He seemed as guileless

as I remembered him, coaxing his mower
like a push toy over the curb at the edge

of his driveway. I knew his family.
His son had grown up to be municipal surveyor

and I had heard that his wife was remarried,
was it to a pharmacist in Oakville?

No sign of the drowning, no bloating.
He still had on the khaki safari jacket

they found him in, two sizes too big,
but laundered now and with none

of the stones dragging on the pockets,
only some loose change that he jingled.

In his basket was a bag of flour, an apple,
a package of ground beef, some muesli.

He saw I was only buying cream
and asked if I wanted to go in front.

Jacob

When I find you in my dream I keep looking
for the hold on you as my own, and you,
always on the verge of parting, say to me

I am the way, follow me, not moving
to all appearance, doing your part
in that inscrutable way you leave me

to find. I say *When you appear like this*
on your own to move me, there is a way
I feel you leave me that I cannot follow.

And you say *Dreamer, I come as I am.*
Surely you can feel it. Follow that.
And I say, *I want to move you that way*

myself. And I move to touch the hollow
of your thigh, and press on the socket
where your hip is, but you turn your thigh

and lay your hand against me, and say
Is that the way you are? Come now.
You're dreaming and I feel for you.

See here, you have to let me go
—it's the only way—if you want to keep
one you love from leaving you

the way you are. I am the way I am.
Do you follow me? And I say *I see.*
So I take the part of me in hand that moves

the way it does, and it moves, and you feel
for it. You say *Like that now, if you follow me,*
follow me. And I feel how you move me

as the dream gives way. I almost think
I hear you say my name, though it is
nothing for you to leave me when you go.

Leper Bell

for K.

I keep trying to come at this
from a different angle, but each time

the clapper that chimes distantly
and with each step grows

more audible is all you can listen for,
like the word at the end of a poem,

almost out of hearing, the hard-thing-
to-say's tintinnabulum.

If I were closer to you than I am,
and if you could hear me over the sound

of the bell, I would want to say something,
for instance, about your skin and how

I feel about it, its colour to begin with,
and a word about its lithesome nap.

And as I came nearer and spoke,
I would have you hear only a more

promising bell's familiar accompaniment,
a clay-bones' bated scuttle above your door,

or the four-note bubble of wood chimes
on the porch where we would sit,

or from across town the giddy carillon's cajoling
try-as-you-may at the wedding chapel.

Not this single bell, sole metaphor
that hangs around the neck of a love poem

that has something it needs to tell you,
the old, heartfelt jingle, still far away.

Pangaea

The continents are distant now
and seem like separate places.

Not that they fell out of love,
as many have thought.

They simply drifted apart.
And with how little bitterness

or animosity it is hard for us
to imagine. We, who have not

yet learned how to part ways,
are corrected by what must have been

their enduring patience, measured
by a mind-trick's time-lapse

portrait of millennia, turned
to abbreviated eras.

Each still has a spoon shape
that holds the other like a memory.

The mountains on both sides stand
undiminished, and the open shores

where they ripped share to this day
a reddish soil washed regularly clean.

There were little faults
and their alienation grew by inches

until a distant line was left thinly
scrawled where the other slipped away.

But when we let fall a lover's hand
for the last time, we leave poised

between reaching fingers a brief abyss
for astonished seconds.

We skirt vast continents in hours
and never see as scars the beaches

that we gravitate towards, or guess that,
after parting years, the empty spaces

between them, mild and grey-rinsed
for this morning's drift of dreaming

first-time lovers, hand in hand,
would need so much healing water.

Twice Over

You are not ready to read this. Just saying.
All that reading is is getting ready to read.
Reading is reconnaissance, reading is a probe.

This poem you have opened to and begun,
let me try to guess what you're after.
You want to know what it's like, what instruction

you will find here, what delight. That is, if you
decide to read it again properly and for real.
You say: this is what it will feel like reading this

when I get round to reading it. You think ahead.
It is like peering through a restaurant window
before you enter it, or like meeting a woman

as she speaks to a friend about a recent book,
not really noticing you, and you listen in, knowing
that you'll think of something to say only later.

But also not that, because of course you *are* reading
this poem, and have got at least as far as you have,
if no farther. You are not just thinking of reading it.

It is, rather, like seeing a landscape for the first time,
for instance, a winter meadow with hard grasses
sifting the snow and a little frozen creek, and you

walk out into it, and as you walk you imagine
a day in the future when you will make the hour
part of a story you share with others, saying

'There were days I used to go out walking
in the snow among the grasses as far as the creek.'
How deeply moved you will feel telling it like that,

the day when your readying turned to readiness.
Which is why perhaps you should say to yourself,
as you read these lines, 'I once read this poem

about reading and how we are never quite ready
to read. I found it hard to follow and never really
went back to it. But I think there was a meadow.'

Acknowledgements

Sincere thanks to the editors of the following journals, who were kind enough to publish earlier versions of poems contained here: *The Fiddlehead, Arc, Alabama Review*.

Many thanks to the Ontario Arts Council for their 'Work in Progress' and 'Writers' Reserve' grants.

And to the abiding spirit of Richard Outram, who brought my editor Amanda Jernigan and her husband John Haney into my life.

About the Poet

Jeffery Donaldson is the author of four previous collections of poetry, most recently *Guesswork*. *Palilalia* was a finalist for the Canadian Authors' Association Award for Poetry. He teaches poetry and American literature at McMaster University in Hamilton. He lives in Stoney Creek.

A Note About the Type

In 1926, under the direction of Heinrich Jost, Louis Höll cut the punches for a new version of Bodoni to be offered for sale by the storied Bauer typefoundry of Frankfurt am Main. Bodoni was originally designed by and named after Giambattista Bodoni of Parma, Italy, who designed his famous types at the end of the eighteenth century. Bauer Bodoni is thought to be closest to the original Bodoni both in its proportions and in its characteristic refinement and delicacy. Bodoni is one of the signifiers of the so-called modern style of type design, with its characteristic difference in thick and thin letter strokes, severe vertical stress, and extremely fine, delicate serifs and hairlines.